The Bombing of
Pearl Harbor

Sabrina Crewe and Michael V. Uschan

Gareth Stevens Publishing
A WORLD ALMANAC EDUCATION GROUP COMPANY

To Gaël Mustapha

Please visit our web site at: www.garethstevens.com
For a free color catalog describing Gareth Stevens Publishing's list of high-quality books and multimedia programs, call 1-800-542-2595 (USA) or 1-800-387-3178 (Canada). Gareth Stevens Publishing's fax: (414) 332-3567.

Library of Congress Cataloging-in-Publication Data

Crewe, Sabrina.
    The bombing of Pearl Harbor / by Sabrina Crewe and Michael V. Uschan.
       p. cm. — (Events that shaped America)
    Includes bibliographical references and index.
    ISBN 0-8368-3392-9 (lib. bdg.)
    1. Pearl Harbor (Hawaii), Attack on, 1941—Juvenile literature. 2. World War, 1939-1945—
Causes—Juvenile literature. 3. United States—Foreign relations—Japan—Juvenile literature.
4. Japan—Foreign relations—United States—Juvenile literature. [1. Pearl Harbor (Hawaii),
Attack on, 1941. 2. World War, 1939-1945—Causes.] I. Uschan, Michael V., 1948- .
II. Title. III. Series.
    D767.92.C76   2003
    940.54'26—dc21   2002030995

First published in 2003 by
Gareth Stevens Publishing
A World Almanac Education Group Company
330 West Olive Street, Suite 100
Milwaukee, WI 53212 USA

Copyright © 2003 by Gareth Stevens Publishing.

Produced by Discovery Books
Editor: Sabrina Crewe
Designer and page production: Sabine Beaupré
Photo researcher: Sabrina Crewe
Maps and diagrams: Stefan Chabluk
Gareth Stevens editorial direction: Mark J. Sachner
Gareth Stevens art direction: Tammy Gruenewald
Gareth Stevens production: Jessica Yanke

Photo credits: Corbis: pp. 6, 7, 9, 10, 11, 13, 15, 16, 18, 20, 21 (both), 22, 23, 24, 25, 26; The Granger Collection: cover; USS *Arizona* Memorial, National Park Service, Photo Collection: pp. 4, 5, 14, 17, 19, 27.

Printed in the United States of America

1 2 3 4 5 6 7 8 9 07 06 05 04 03

Contents

Introduction

This is a photograph taken from a Japanese plane attacking Pearl Harbor. Battleship Row, where the biggest ships were anchored, is in the foreground.

Attack on the United States

On December 7, 1941, something happened that changed the United States forever. That morning, Japanese planes swooped in over the island of Oahu in Hawaii and attacked Pearl Harbor, an American military base. Their bombs blew up ships and planes and buildings.

The attack on Pearl Harbor only lasted two hours, but it was a terrible and shocking event. It was also very sad because 2,388 Americans died and 1,178 people were wounded.

A World War

The attack on Pearl Harbor was part of the worldwide conflict that took place during World War II. By December 1941, World War II had been raging for several years. There was fighting in Asia, in Europe, and in Africa. Millions of people—soldiers and **civilians**—had been killed. The United States, however, had stayed out of the war because many Americans felt it had nothing to do with them.

Going into World War II

After Japan attacked Pearl Harbor, Americans changed their minds. They were horrified and angry, and they wanted revenge. They also realized that the United States could not ignore what was happening in the rest of the world.

The day after Japanese planes bombed Pearl Harbor, the United States declared war on Japan. President Franklin D. Roosevelt said that December 7, 1941, would be "a date which will live in **infamy**." This turned out to be true. The attack happened more than sixty years ago, which seems like a very long time. But there are still people alive who were there on that awful day. They can remind us of the horror that war brings to people's lives.

A Date Which Will Live in Infamy

"Yesterday, December 7, 1941—a date which will live in infamy—the United States of America was suddenly and deliberately attacked by naval and air forces of the Empire of Japan. . . . No matter how long it may take us to overcome this premeditated invasion, the American people in their righteous might will win through to absolute victory."

President Franklin D. Roosevelt, December 8, 1941, in a speech asking Congress to declare war on Japan

These men were all serving at Pearl Harbor when it was attacked in 1941. They returned to Hawaii in December 2001 for the sixtieth anniversary of the attack.

Chapter One

War Around the World

Adolf Hitler, leader of Germany's powerful Nazi Party, stands with other Nazis at a rally. The Nazis caused the death of millions of people during World War II.

The Axis Powers

There were many reasons for World War II, but they really boil down to certain nations or people wanting power over other nations or people. Throughout history, this has been the reason for many wars.

In World War II, the nations that were trying to seize power were Germany, Italy, and Japan. Germany and Italy were led by fascists, and Japan was run by a military government. These leaders were using their armies and navies to take over other countries, hoping to increase the wealth and power of their own nations. In 1940, Japan, Germany, and Italy got together to sign an agreement. Together, they were called the Axis Powers.

Fascism

This is what fascists believe:
> Their country is better than anyone else's, and their race or people, are superior.
> The government, and especially the leader, should be completely in charge of citizens.
> Nobody is allowed to disagree with the government.

The Allies

On the other side of the war, there were many more countries—known as the **Allies**—trying to fight back against the Axis. The trouble was that some of the Allies in Europe had already been invaded by Germany, and Hitler had spent much of 1940 attacking France and Britain. Meanwhile, Japan had invaded China in 1937 and wanted to conquer the rest of the Far East (the countries of Asia in and around the Pacific Ocean).

Isolationists

In the agreement they signed in 1940, the Axis Powers had promised to help each other if any one of them was attacked by the United States. Most Americans, however, did not want to attack anyone or get involved in the war at all. They were **isolationists**, which means they wanted to stay isolated—or separate—from trouble in the rest of the world.

An Early Isolationist
"'Tis your true **policy** to steer clear of permanent Alliances, with any portion of the foreign World."

George Washington, the nation's first president, advises Americans to be isolationists in his farewell address in 1797

Japanese troops march into Nanking, then capital of China, in the invasion of 1937. Japanese leaders believed their nation should take control of Asia.

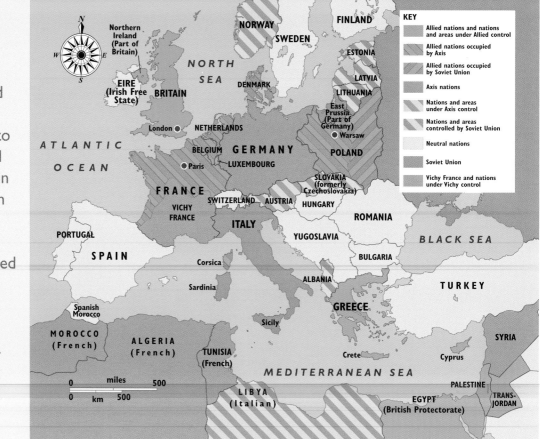

This map shows how Europe and North Africa were divided into Allied, Axis, and neutral nations in 1940. In addition to the nations shown here, Canada had joined the Allies, but the United States was still a neutral nation.

KEY

- Allied nations and nations and areas under Allied control
- Allied nations occupied by Axis
- Allied nations occupied by Soviet Union
- Axis nations
- Nations and areas under Axis control
- Nations and areas controlled by Soviet Union
- Neutral nations
- Soviet Union
- Vichy France and nations under Vichy control

FDR's Presidency

In reality, however, Americans were helping the Allies. This was because the president, Franklin D. Roosevelt, was an **interventionist**. He believed that if the powerful United States did nothing to help its allies, the Axis would conquer the world. That would be dangerous for Americans as well as for everyone else. So Roosevelt made sure his nation helped by lending ships, planes, and weapons to Britain and China. He also persuaded Congress to spend a lot of money—$17 billion— to build up the U.S. Army and U.S. Navy.

Remaining Neutral

What President Roosevelt couldn't do was to make the United States enter the war against the wishes

of the people. That's because the United States of America
is a democracy, and the U.S. government is there to represent
its citizens. Even the most powerful man in the country has
to get Congress—which represents American citizens—to
agree before going to war.

The United States was strengthening its military so it
could protect itself in case of attack. Most Americans sided
with the Allies, but they were still not ready to go to war
themselves to stop Germany and Japan. In 1941, the United
States remained a **neutral** country in a world at war.

Workers at this factory in Akron, Ohio, are making antiaircraft guns for use during World War II. Before the war, this plant had been a tire factory.

Chapter Two

In the Pacific

American Interests in the Pacific

The United States was staying out of World War II, but it still had interests in the Pacific, where Japan was trying to take control. Among these was Hawaii, a group of eight islands about 2,400 miles (about 4,000 kilometers) west of San Francisco. Way out in the Pacific Ocean, Hawaii was at the time a **U.S. Territory.** (Now, of course, it is a state.) The islands were important ports for American ships traveling to the Far East to trade with China and other nations. Hawaii also made money for Americans with its sugar crop.

The United States had important ties with other countries in the Far East, too, such as China. Because of this, the United States was getting very worried about what Japan was doing there.

Sugar is still an important crop in Hawaii. These are sugarcane fields in Hawaii today.

President Roosevelt Acts

In 1940, President Roosevelt feared that Japan was going to attack more nations in the Pacific. So, in May, he moved the headquarters for the U.S. Navy's Pacific **Fleet** from California to Hawaii. The headquarters were now on the island of Oahu, at Pearl Harbor. Halfway between the United States and the Far East, Pearl Harbor became a very important place.

Franklin Delano Roosevelt (1882–1945)

President Franklin D. Roosevelt making a radio broadcast.

Franklin Delano Roosevelt, the nation's thirty-second president, was born in New York in 1882. In 1921, when he was thirty-nine years old, Roosevelt got polio, which is a horrible disease that attacks people's muscles. He soon needed crutches to walk and then, as he grew older, used a wheelchair. In spite of this, Roosevelt served as governor of New York and was elected president in 1932. He served longer than any other U.S. president, from March 4, 1933, until his death on April 12, 1945. Roosevelt is often considered to be one of the greatest, most important presidents in U.S. history. He helped the United States survive the Great Depression of the 1920s and 1930s and helped the Allies defeat Japan and Germany in World War II. Roosevelt died just before the end of the war.

This map shows where the Hawaiian Islands are. The areas in pink were those controlled by Japan in 1941.

Heading Toward War

To the Japanese, it appeared that the United States was threatening their country. The commander of the Japanese navy, Japanese Admiral Isoroku Yamamoto, was especially worried about the U.S. ships stationed in Pearl Harbor. He said the naval base was "a dagger being pointed at our throat." In 1941, President Roosevelt stopped Americans from selling oil, steel, or other war supplies to Japan. This greatly angered the Japanese, who needed those supplies to invade other countries.

In October, General Hideki Tojo became Japan's prime minister. He decided to fight the United States. Tojo's first step toward war was to approve a daring plan by Admiral Yamamoto to cripple the Pacific Fleet by attacking Pearl Harbor with planes launched from aircraft carriers. To be successful, the attack would have to be a surprise. Japanese

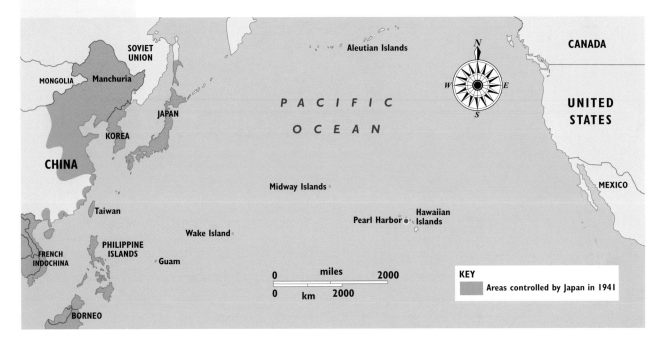

diplomats in Washington, D.C., started talks with American officials. They pretended they wanted to discuss peace when, in fact, they were planning to bomb Pearl Harbor.

Pearl Harbor

Pearl Harbor took its name from the many oysters, containing pearls, that Hawaiians find in its waters. Hawaiians called the area *Wai Momi*, which means "pearl waters." Pearl Harbor is six miles (10 km) west of the city of Honolulu. It is a large harbor, with 10 square miles (26 square kilometers) of water deep enough and wide enough for big ships such as battleships to enter. Pearl Harbor Naval Station also has 10,000 acres (4,000 hectares) of land. This includes Ford Island, in the middle of the harbor, which had a base for military airplanes in 1941. The navy had many buildings around the harbor. These were houses, warehouses, training centers, offices, and a hospital. There were also yards to repair ships.

Pearl Harbor today, with Ford Island visible in the center right beyond the mainland.

Lieutenant General Walter Short (left) and Admiral Husband Kimmel (right) were in command of Pearl Harbor when it was attacked in December 1941. They are seen here with British Admiral Louis Mountbatten (center).

A Warning of War

U.S. officials soon figured out that the Japanese were not as friendly as they seemed. Messages in secret code went back and forth between Japan and their diplomats in Washington, D.C. Unknown to Japan, U.S. **intelligence** officials had developed a machine—nicknamed "Magic"—that allowed them to read the messages.

In November 1941, the messages showed that the Japanese were not going to agree to American terms for peace. This probably meant war. So, on November 27, officials in Washington issued a "war warning" to the U.S. Navy and Army in the Pacific. In Hawaii, the warnings went to Admiral Husband E. Kimmel, commander of the Pacific Fleet, and Lieutenant General Walter Short, who commanded ground forces there.

Expecting Aggression

"This dispatch is to be considered a war warning: Negotiations with Japan have ceased and an aggressive move by Japan is expected within the next few days. Japanese troops and naval task forces indicate an . . . expedition against either the Philippines, Thailand . . . or possibly Borneo. Execute an appropriate defensive **deployment**."

Admiral Harold R. Stark, part of the war warning issued November 27, 1941

At the time, however, American officials thought that if the Japanese attacked the United States, it would be somewhere else in the Pacific. This created a false sense of security that led Kimmel and Short to feel they were safe.

A Fatal Delay

On December 6, 1941, intelligence agents decoded part of a long message from Japan to its diplomats. It said Japan would not agree to what the United States was asking. "This means war," Roosevelt said. On Sunday morning, December 7, realizing that Japan might attack any moment, the War Department issued a new warning.

The warning did not reach Pearl Harbor in time. Military leaders still did not believe Pearl Harbor would be attacked, and so they didn't deliver the warning immediately. By the time the message arrived at U.S. Army headquarters on Oahu, the attack was over.

A view of the Pearl Harbor naval base as it was in the quiet days before the attack. Two submarines can be seen at the dock.

15

Chapter Three

The Attack on Pearl Harbor

The Japanese Fleet Arrives

The Japanese **aircraft carrier** *Akagi* was one of a fleet of thirty-three ships that left Japan on November 26, 1941. The fleet crossed 4,000 miles (6,400 km) of open sea to a spot 220 miles (350 km) north of Oahu.

The Planes Take Off

Before dawn on December 7, 1941, a wave of 183 Japanese war planes took off from the *Akagi* and began flying toward Pearl Harbor. Thirty minutes later, a second group of 167 planes was launched. Japanese bomber pilot Abe Zenji remembered how

Early on December 7, 1941, a group of Japanese pilots and sailors wave as a bomber gets ready to leave for the attack on Pearl Harbor. A Japanese flag flies on the mast.

This picture, taken from a Japanese war plane, shows Ford Island in the opening moments of the attack. The *Oklahoma* has just been bombed—you can see a plume of water spurting up from the battleship where it was hit.

the planes looked as they flew away: "It was like the sky was filled with fireflies."

No one at Pearl Harbor knew they were coming. The attack would be a total surprise to the 100,000 American soldiers and sailors stationed on Oahu.

At 7:52 A.M., the first planes roared over Oahu. Their pilots saw the harbor that, from the sky, looked like a piece from a giant jigsaw puzzle. In the center was Ford Island, where the naval air station lay. Next to Ford Island was Battleship Row, where the navy's biggest ships lay side by side. More than ninety battleships, destroyers, cruisers, and support ships were anchored that day in Pearl Harbor.

Taken by Surprise
"I'm standing there eating an apple on the deck of the *Argonne* when suddenly dive-bombers hit out of the blue! You knew they were Japanese because they had those big red symbols on the front—we called them meatballs. We stood there with our mouths open, watching the **hangars** [on Ford Island] blowing up!"

Joseph Ryan, a navy radio operator

The *Oklahoma* Goes Down

"The thing that really sticks in my mind was the *Oklahoma* beginning to roll. She had a big explosion, and a hatch came off and went up in the air. . . . We had been told all our lives that you couldn't sink a battleship, and then to see one go upside down . . . it's heartbreaking. I knew how many were on the ship. I had a lot of shipmates there . . . and I knew they had gone down inside."

Gunner's Mate Third Class George Waller, who was on the battleship Maryland *anchored next to the* Oklahoma

Bombing the Ships

The first bombs fell at 7:55 A.M. In just a few minutes, the battleships *West Virginia*, *Oklahoma*, and *California* were all hit and sinking. The battleships were the main target, but smaller vessels were also damaged or destroyed.

At about 8:10 A.M., a huge bomb hit the deck of the *Arizona*. It set off a tremendous explosion that sent a smoky fireball soaring high above the ship. In only nine minutes, the *Arizona* sank with 1,177 of her crew. Nearly half the Americans killed that day were on the *Arizona*.

Sailors try to escape the sinking *California*, one of the first battleships to be hit in the attack. But the water around them is dangerous, too, because of burning oil on its surface.

This is a photograph of the huge explosion set off by the giant bomb that hit the battleship *Arizona*.

Within a few minutes, the peaceful harbor was aflame. Dense clouds of black, oily smoke rose into the blue Hawaiian sky. Oil that spilled out of the damaged ships caught fire, creating walls of flame on the open sea. Sailors who jumped into the water from sinking ships to escape death were burned horribly by the oil.

A Hero in a Sinking Ship

Many sailors drowned because they were below decks when ships sank. In the *Oklahoma*, four men were trapped as water flooded in. The four sailors located a porthole through which they could escape. One of them, Chief Carpenter Arnold Austin, was too big to get through the porthole, so he held it open for the others. He helped them to safety even though he knew he would die.

After the Bomb

"But after the second or third bomb—I don't know which—that hit the *Arizona* . . . I wound up over the side of the *Arizona* in the water. . . . There were steel fragments in the air, fire, oil . . . pieces of timber, pieces of the boat deck, canvas, and even pieces of bodies."

Martin Matthews, a fifteen-year-old sailor in training on Ford Island, who was on board the Arizona *when the attack began*

A fireball rises above one of the airfields that were attacked at Pearl Harbor. There was no way to protect the airplanes laid out in rows on the airfields.

Other Targets

Pearl Harbor was the main target, but Japanese planes struck the Oahu airfields, too. Their goal was to destroy U.S. planes. The pilots also fired their machine guns and killed many men racing around on the airfields below them.

Shortly before 10 A.M., the last Japanese planes flew back to their carriers. After two hours, the attack was finally over.

An Appalling Sight

"The sight that met our eyes was appalling. Thick, black smoke was spiraling skyward from all over the basin. Battleship Row was a shambles. Everything was in a state of total confusion."

Navy Radio Operator Harry R. Mead, describing his return to Ford Island from an unsuccessful attempt to locate the enemy fleet by plane during the attack

Dorie Miller (1919–1943)

One of the men who bravely fought back was Doris (Dorie) Miller, a twenty-two-year-old sailor from Waco, Texas, who was a cook's assistant. He manned a machine gun on his ship even though he not been trained. He kept firing at enemy planes until heat and flames from the burning ship forced him to leap into the ocean along with other sailors. Because of what he did, Miller was given the Navy Cross, a medal for heroes.

The Navy Cross

Fighting Back

As the bombs fell, sailors on board ship rushed to their battle stations. So did soldiers and airmen on land. They began firing machine guns and antiaircraft guns. The enemy planes flew so low that Americans could see the faces of their attackers. Some pilots even waved at the men they were trying to kill.

Only fourteen U.S. pilots managed to get into the air, but among them, they managed to shoot down eleven enemy planes. The men on the battleship *Nevada*, already badly damaged, tried to leave the harbor to fight back. But they stopped when they realized the ship might sink and block the harbor entrance.

The United States in World War II

Chapter Five

This poster was used during World War II to encourage citizens and members of the military in their war effort.

...we here highly resolve that these dead shall not have died in vain...

REMEMBER DEC. 7th!

Repairing the Damage

Pearl Harbor was a huge disaster for the U.S. Navy. There were 21 ships sunk or damaged and 164 planes destroyed. Over the next few months, however, the navy raised sunken ships and repaired its fleet. Within a few months, Pearl Harbor was ready for war.

A Declaration of War

The tragedy of Pearl Harbor had immediately united the nation against Japan. On December 8, President Franklin D. Roosevelt asked Congress to declare war against Japan, and the United States entered World War II.

The Allies faced a huge task because the Japanese had started a mighty **offensive** across the South Pacific. In the summer of 1942, however, the tide turned. The United States won the Battle of the Coral Sea and the Battle of Midway. From then until the end of the war, the Japanese retreated as the Allies advanced.

24

This is what Hiroshima looked like after the atomic bomb was dropped on the city in 1945. More than 160,000 people died or were injured.

The Atomic Bomb

Over the next three years, the Allies continued to fight in World War II. Germany surrendered in May 1945, ending World War II in Europe. The Allies now focused on Japan. By this time, the United States had a new president, Harry S. Truman, because Roosevelt had died in April.

The United States also had a new weapon, the atomic bomb. It was the most destructive weapon the world had ever known. On August 6, 1945, the United States dropped an atomic bomb on Hiroshima, Japan, killing about eighty thousand people. When Japan refused to surrender, another bomb was dropped on the Japanese city of Nagasaki. The second bomb, on August 9, killed more than forty thousand people. On August 14, 1945, Japan surrendered, and World War II was over. No atomic bombs had ever been used in war before, and none has been since.

Using the Bomb

"Having found the bomb we have used it. We have used it against those who attacked us without warning at Pearl Harbor. We have used it in order to shorten the agony of war, in order to save the lives of thousands and thousands of young Americans. We shall continue to use it until we completely destroy Japan's power to make war."

President Harry S. Truman explaining why he decided to use the atomic bomb on Japan

Conclusion

Why Wasn't Pearl Harbor Ready?

After Pearl Harbor, Congress and the military blamed the commanders in Hawaii for not preventing the attack. They said Admiral Kimmel and General Short had not been ready. Official reports stated that they had failed to protect their men. Much later, the government came to realize that a lot of other people were at fault. Mistakes had been made, and there was a bad lack of communication between Washington, D.C., and the Pacific. That is why Pearl Harbor was not prepared for the Japanese attack.

Japanese Americans

In 1942, the U.S. government forced 110,000 people of Japanese descent to move to prison camps. Some officials believed Japanese Americans were a danger to the United States during World War II because they would take Japan's side. The **internment** was very unfair because most of the people involved were loyal American citizens. After the attack on Pearl Harbor, thousands of Japanese Americans joined the military and fought for the United States.

The Hirano family photographed in an internment camp with a picture of their family member who joined the military to fight in World War II.

The *Arizona* Memorial rests across the deck of the sunken battleship. About 1.5 million visitors come to see it every year.

Pearl Harbor Today

Pearl Harbor is still an important military base. Today, it is home to more than 81,000 members of the military and their families. Pearl Harbor is like a small city with its housing, churches, stores, and schools.

On Memorial Day in 1962, a memorial was opened that had been built on the deck of the battleship *Arizona*. The memorial honors all those who were killed December 7, 1941, but especially the 1,177 sailors who died aboard the *Arizona*.

The memorial also reminds us of the lesson of Pearl Harbor. The attack forced Americans to end their isolationism. In order to survive in the future, the United States would have to ally itself with other nations. It would also need to play an active role in world affairs in times of international crisis.

Citizens of the World

"We have learned that we cannot live alone, at peace; that our well-being is dependent on the well-being of other nations, far away. We have learned to be citizens of the world, members of the [global] community."

President Franklin D. Roosevelt, January 20, 1945

Time Line

1937   Japan invades China.

1939   September 1: German troops invade Poland to begin World War II in Europe.

1940   May: Headquarters of U.S. Navy's Pacific Fleet is moved to Pearl Harbor.

June: Germany occupies France.

September: Japan, Germany, and Italy sign Tripartite Pact.

November 7: Franklin Delano Roosevelt is reelected as U.S. president.

1941   March: Congress passes Lend-Lease Act, which provides supplies to nations fighting Axis Powers.

July 25: Roosevelt bans shipments of scrap iron and gasoline to Japan.

December 7: Japan attacks Pearl Harbor.

December 8: The United States declares war on Japan.

1942   February: Roosevelt signs order to intern Japanese Americans.

May 4–8: Battle of the Coral Sea.

June 4–6: Battle of Midway.

1945   April 12: Roosevelt dies, and Harry S. Truman becomes president.

May 7: Germany surrenders to Allies.

August 6: United States drops atomic bomb on Hiroshima, Japan.

August 9: United States drops atomic bomb on Nagasaki, Japan.

August 14: Japan surrenders to Allies, ending World War II.

1962   Memorial Day: Memorial dedicated on USS *Arizona* in Pearl Harbor.

Things to Think About and Do

An Occupied Country

At the beginning of World War II, fascist leaders in Europe invaded other nations because they wanted more land and power. Imagine you lived in Poland or France when the German military forces took over your country. Find out more about what it was like to live in one of these countries during World War II, and write a couple of paragraphs describing how your life suddenly changed after the invasion.

Making the Choice

Imagine you were alive in 1941, just before the United States entered World War II. Would you be an isolationist, as many people were then, or an interventionist, as President Roosevelt and others were? Give a few reasons for your choice. What would you choose to be today if a similar problem arose?

The Attack

Imagine you are a nurse or sailor stationed at Pearl Harbor in 1941. Write three diary entries for the days just before, during, and just after the bombing of Pearl Harbor by the Japanese.

Internment

During World War II, Japanese Americans were considered a threat to security even though they were American citizens. Do you think the government was wrong or right to imprison them? Give your reasons why. What would you think if a certain group of Americans was imprisoned today because they happened to be of a certain race or religion?

Glossary

aircraft carrier:	large ship with a long flat deck on which planes can take off and land.
allies:	People or groups or countries that agree to support and defend each other.
civilian:	person who is not in the armed forces.
deployment:	positioning of military forces and equipment.
diplomat:	person who represents his or her country in another country.
fleet:	group of ships under a single command. In World War II, the Pacific Fleet was the U.S. Navy's entire naval force in and around the Pacific Ocean.
hangar:	building for housing aircraft.
hull:	body and sides of a ship.
infamy:	fame of a bad kind, such as that of a terrible event or person.
intelligence:	information about enemies or enemy actions. Intelligence officers are people whose job is to find out as much as they can about enemies or possible enemies and what they are doing.
internment:	holding of people in prison-like conditions, usually in wartime.
interventionist:	person who gets involved or interferes in something. In World War II, it meant a person who believed the United States should help defend nations attacked by fascist nations.
isolationist:	person who believes his or her nation should not get involved in the conflicts of other nations.
neutral:	not taking sides in a conflict.
offensive:	large, planned attack.
policy:	plan or way of doing things that is decided upon and then used in managing situations and making decisions.
U.S. Territory:	geographical area that belongs to and is governed by the United States but is not included in any of its states.

Further Information

Books

Allen, Thomas B. and Robert D. Ballard. *Remember Pearl Harbor: American and Japanese Survivors Tell Their Stories*. National Geographic Society, 2001.

Denenberg, Barry. *Early Sunday Morning: The Pearl Harbor Diary of Amber Billows, Hawaii, 1941* (Dear America). Scholastic, 2001.

King, David C. *World War II Days: Discover the Past with Exciting Projects, Games, Activities, and Recipes* (American Kids in History). John Wiley and Sons, 2000.

Spies, Karen Bornemann. *Franklin D. Roosevelt* (United States Presidents). Enslow, 1999.

Stanley, Jerry. *I Am an American: A True Story of Japanese Internment*. Crown, 1996.

Web Sites

www.arizonamemorial.org/pearlharbor Good information and pictures presented by the *Arizona* Memorial Museum Association, dedicated to the history of the attack on Pearl Harbor.

www.nps.gov/usar Web site of the National Park Service that runs the *Arizona* Memorial in Pearl Harbor.

plasma.nationalgeographic.com/pearlharbor/ National Geographic web site is full of information, pictures, and animated material relating to Pearl Harbor.

Useful Addresses

USS *Arizona* Memorial
National Park Service
1 Arizona Memorial Place
Honolulu, HI 96818
Telephone: (808) 422-0561

Index

Page numbers in **bold** indicate pictures.